Writing
Strands

A COMPLETE WRITING PROGRAM
USING A PROCESS APPROACH
TO WRITING AND COMPOSITION

ASSURING
CONTINUITY AND CONTROL

LEVEL 6
of

A WRITING PROGRAM FOR

HOMESCHOOLERS

a
publication
of

NATIONAL WRITING INSTITUTE
624 W. University #248
Denton, TX 76201-1889

ISBN 1-888344-06-7

Manufactured in the United States of America

For information write   National Writing Institute,
                          624 W University #248
                          Denton TX 76201-1889

                          Call: 800 688-5375
                          Fax: 940 3834414
                          e-mail, info@writingstrands.com

NATIONAL WRITING INSTITUTE PUBLICATIONS
and
SERVICE

STUDENTS

Writing Strands Level 1
Writing Strands Level 2
Writing Strands Level 3
Writing Strands Level 4
Writing Strands Level 5
Writing Strands Level 6
Writing Strands Level 7
Writing Exposition
Creating Fiction

Communication And Interpersonal Relationships

FICTION

Dragonslaying Is For Dreamers
Axel Meets The Blue Men
Axel's Challenge

———

PARENTS/TEACHERS

Evaluating Writing
Reading Strands
Analyzing The Novel:
Dragonslaying Is For Dreamers

———

SERVICES FOR PARENTS

Evaluation Program

INTRODUCTION

This group of exercises is designed to give sixth level students (generally advanced high school students who haven't used *Writing Strands*, or any student who has finished level five *Writing Strands*), an introduction to the very complicated process of giving others their thoughts in written form.

The learning of this skill is one of the hardest jobs that you have. These exercises will make it easier. Much of the planning and detail of the writing process is presented here.

The writing exercises in this level are in three categories: creative, research and report, and expository. The exercises in each of these areas will guide you in the development of the skills you will need.

Rather than increase the work for your parents, this writing process should make it easier for both you and your parents to meet the demands for more student writing.

These exercises are not presented as the ultimate answer. They're detailed suggestions. If the exercises are attempted and you work hard, you will have a well-founded introduction to this most difficult skill, and your parents will find it easier to have confidence that this part of the teaching challenge has been met.

CONTENTS

page

HOW TO MAKE

WRITING STRANDS WORK FOR YOU

1. You should have a writing folder containing all of your written work which should be saved for next year. This will give you a place to store and record your progress, and it's a great thing for your parents to keep.

2. Both semesters' work have evaluations by your parents which may be used if your parents have to have a conference with your local school administration. They contain:
   1) The objectives you have mastered this year;
   2) A place for your parents to comment on your work and a place to list the things you have yet to learn.

3. Each exercise begins with a suggested time for completion. Of course, all students work at different rates. The suggested daily activities can be combined or extended depending on your performance and your parents' schedules.

4. Many of the exercises suggest that your parents will work with you during your schooling period reading what you have written. If this is done, it will serve two purposes:
   1) It will give you constant feedback and will allow your parents to catch many writing problems before they appear in your final papers.
   2) It will greatly cut down on your parents' correcting time outside of your working periods. Most of the paper reading can be done while you're working on language arts, so, even though you will be writing much more than you previously have been, your parents should be able to help you more using even less outside time.

5. At the end of each semester's work there is an evaluation form that should list the continuing problems you have:
   1) The form at the end of the first semester should contain a listing of the problems that you should work on during the second semester.
   2) The year's-end evaluation form should list the problems that you will be able to solve next year.

PRINCIPLES

The following principles were adopted by the National Writing Institute before work began on *Writing Strands*. They were our guides in the initial stages of the design of the exercises.

1. Every person needs to learn to express ideas and feelings through writing.

2. There is no one right way to write anything.

3. The ability to write isn't an expression of a body of knowledge that can be learned like a list of vocabulary words.

4. Writing teachers and their students both learn in any effective writing situation.

5. The product of each student's writing efforts must be seen as a success for at least the following reasons:
   1) A student in a writing experience isn't in competition with anyone else.
   2) There is no perfect model against which any effort can be compared for evaluation, so there is no best way for any student to write.
   3) Every controlled writing experience will help students improve the ability to express themselves.

6. All student writing efforts are worthy of praise. The most help any writing teacher can give at any point is to show, in a positive way, what is good about a piece and how it might be improved.

7. Any writing lesson assigned, which is done independently by a student and doesn't have a teacher's constant feedback in the form of reinforcement and suggestions, represents a missed opportunity for the student.

8. All writing at any level is hard work, and every writer should be encouraged to feel the pride of authorship.

9. All authors need to be published. This can be accomplished by having their work read to family members, posted on the bulletin board, printed in "books" or stuck on the front of the refrigerator.

SIXTH LEVEL

EXERCISES * SKILLS * OBJECTIVES

Exercise 1: Body Control
Skill Area: Creative

1. Accepting that adults are better than teenagers at controlling their body movements
2. Using this knowledge in writing

Exercise 2: If I Were a . . .
Skill Strand: Research and Report

1. Understanding that the things we call good and bad are determined by who we are
2. Realizing that ideas may be looked at in more than one way
3. Understanding that the organization of a report should help the reader understand it

Exercise 3: Conflict
Skill Strand: Creative

1. Understanding that conflict is one of the things that makes reading stories fun
2. Creating conflicts in writing

Exercise 4: Point of View
Skill Strand: Expository

1. Knowing three of the choices an author has in his use of point of view
2. Understanding how these point of view elements work
3. Understanding the structuring of an explanatory exposition
4. Writing an explanatory exposition

Exercise 5: Survey
Skill Strand: Research

1. Writing unbiased questions
2. Selecting a representative sample as respondents to a survey
3. Taking a survey

Exercise 6: Book Report
Skill Strand: Research and Report

1. Identifying the forces in conflict in a novel
2. Describing these forces
3. Showing how these forces are important to the book

Exercise 7: Disorder
Skill Strand: Report

1. Observing a situation and taking notes
2. Describing what has been seen over a period of days
3. Writing a formal scientific report

Exercise 8: Interview With a Character
Skill Strand: Report

1. Understanding that imaginary characters sometimes do what they want to do
2. Writing an interview

Exercise 9: Who Me?
Skill Strand: Creative

1. Recognizing that in some short stories there are stock or stereotypical characters
2. Understanding that some of the characters seen on TV are stock characters
3. Creating both stock characters and characters who have individuality

Exercise 10: Choices of Action
Skill Strand: Creative

1. Describing a personal decision a person might have to make by giving that decision to a character
2. Putting a character in a situation where the reader can see the character trying to make a decision that will be a good one

Exercise 11: Problems
Skill Strand: Creative

1. Constructing an argument between two people
2. Punctuating dialogue
3. Describing, in a dialogue, characters' major body movements caused by their emotional reactions

Exercise 12: Writing Letters
Skill Strand: Organization

1. Understanding the principles of business letters
2. Formatting business letters
3. Writing business letters

STRANDS

Two of the most desired characteristics of any writing program are for it to allow for continuity of instruction from grade to grade and to allow for control of the learning process by the teachers.

Below are the strands, the exercises that present the strands and where they are found in this text.

#1 BODY CONTROL

Sixth Level Skill Strand: Creative

It may take you six days to learn that:
1. Adults are better than teenagers at controlling their body movements.
2. Writers understand this and use it in their writing
3. You can use this understanding in your writing

PREWRITING

Day One:

As they get older, people learn to control their bodies. This isn't a hard thing to do, but it does take practice. If you practice controlling what your body does, people will think you're older than you really are.

Notice how the younger kids you know move their bodies and that this movement has nothing to do with what they're saying or with what they want. Young kids are always jiggling their feet, playing with pencils, twisting hair, chewing gum, scratching or just making random movements with fingers, hands, arms or legs. This is okay, we all did this when we were growing up.

Many of the adults in your life can sit quietly for long periods of time and not show signs of nervousness. Most adults don't have to pick at their hands, bite their fingernails or jiggle their feet—they have learned to control themselves.

In this exercise you will create two characters—one who will be able to control body movements and one who will be young enough not to have learned this. I suggest you put these characters in situations similar to the following:

-A mother talking to her daughter about the daughter picking up her room.

-A father talking to his son about cleaning the garage.

-An adult talking to a child about leaving toys in the yard or bikes in the driveway.

-A parent and a child talking about homeschool.

-A teenager and her mother talking about how nice it would be for the girl to do the dishes for her little brother without expecting anything in return.

-A mother and her daughter waiting for a bus.

-A mother and her child waiting in a doctor's office

Once you have chosen a situation, you should try and visualize it. This means that, like a film, you can run the situation in your mind and "watch" what the two characters do with their bodies.

To help you realize how young people move their bodies in ways that do not help them communicate, watch the kids in your church group or in your youth group. You could keep a listing of their random movements. This does not include gestures, or one-time scratching or shifting of position. Use this page or one like it to keep a record of the kinds of movements you notice.

Random Body Movements

Boy:____ Girl:____ Part of body moved: _____

Pattern of movement:_____

Boy:____ Girl:____ Part of body moved:_____

Pattern of movement:_____

Boy:____ Girl:____ Part of body moved:_____

Pattern of movement:_____

Boy:____ Girl:____ Part of body moved:_____

Pattern of movement:_____

Keep in mind that this exercise is about body control. You should have each character speak at least 15 times. This will give you time to demonstrate how well they both control their bodies.

You will not have to resolve any conflict in this short piece. It will not have to have any structure. It is to give you experience in the different degrees of body control, so, make sure you describe how your characters move as they talk to each other.

Below is a *short* piece of this exercise which you can use as a model. I suggest that you use past tense and a narrative voice which is third person. (If you haven't studied these elements of point of view, turn to the chart on page 18 and the examples that explain how they function.)

Held Over

Bill sat at the kitchen table with his math book open in front of him. He could see through the window across the road to the field where the boys were starting the ball game. He picked up his pencil and put a (1) at the top left corner of his paper. Mrs. Grubber was standing at the sink doing the lunch dishes. When she turned and looked at her son, she saw that he was busy with the thumbnail on his left hand.

Mrs. Grubber sat at the table across from Bill and carefully folded her hands and looked at her son. He looked up at her and noticed that there was a ring of suds on both of her arms. He wiped his own arms of imaginary soap and went back to the nail and began to bounce his right toe off the edge of his chair.

"Bill," said Mrs. Grubber, "sit still. You have fifteen minutes to wait before you can leave."

"Sorry, Mom." He pushed his right toe against his left foot to stop it jumping around and began to pick at an old scab on his left elbow. This was a challenge because he had to twist his arm and pull his skin to see it at all. Just as he got a good look at the scab, he heard his mother clear her throat. He looked up and she was shaking her head. "Sorry, Mom."

Mrs. Grubber took a large breath and let it out slowly, almost as if she were under the soapy water in the sink, and said, "You can control your body if you try, Bill."

"I'll try, Mom," Bill said with sincerity in his voice, and, after a moment, Bill's foot began tapping on the leg of the table.

WRITING

Write a short scenario for your piece. It must be in present tense and have no dialogue or details. It should contain only the major events. Read this short example:

Held Over

Bill Grubber has been told by his mother that he must stay and finish his math before he can play ball with his friends. He has to sit at the kitchen table while his mother is doing the dishes. He has a great deal of trouble concentrating. He picks at his hands and elbow. He taps his feet and looks out the window at his friends. His mother sits at the table and tells him that he's not concentrating and to control his body. He tries and fails.

Day Two:

You should make a list of the body movements of the two characters in your piece. You may use this form if it will help:

BODY MOVEMENTS

Character One (young person):

_____

_____

Character Two (adult):

_____

When your scenario and list of body movements are written and before you start writing your piece, you should ask your parent to look over your work.

Days Three and Four:

Start the piece today. You should plan on having about three pages. When you have a rough draft, you should ask your parent to read it and make suggestions.

Day Five:

Write your second draft and have your parent check it again. When this is done, you should go over your work for spelling and punctuation errors.

Preparation:

You should plan on having your final copy done at the end of day six. Do enough work in the evening so you'll be sure to have your paper done on time.

Day Six:

Your paper should be given to your parent at the end of the session today. You might want to read your paper to family members and have them talk about what they notice about the ways people learn to control their bodies. Your parents should be able to tell you lots about the ways the people at work do this.

I recommend you take the next week off.

PROGRESS REPORT

Name:_____ Date:_____

Exercise # 1 BODY CONTROL

Copy your best sentence for the week on the lines below.

_____

_____

Name one mistake you made this week that you can fix and will avoid next week.

_____

_____

Write the sentence that had this mistake in it.

_____

_____

Write the sentence again showing how you fixed this mistake.

_____

_____

Comments:

#2 IF I WERE A . . .

Sixth Level Skill Strand: Research and Report

It may take you eight days to learn that:
1. Some of the things we call good and bad are determined by who we are
2. Some ideas are looked at in more than one way
3. The organization of a report should help the reader understand it

PREWRITING

Days One and Two:

Most of the disagreements between people come about because of differences in the ways they look at things. This is how some people determine what they call good and bad. The music and the TV programs you like, your parents may not like. You may like fast food or corny jokes and your sister or brother may not. These likes and dislikes are based on taste, which is another word we use to label our likes.

Many beliefs are determined by experiences. If this were not so, we would all believe in the same religions and forms of government. In some places in the world there are people who try and force their beliefs on other people. We are very fortunate here in America that other people cannot force us to believe as they want us to.

If you and I do not like the same things, it doesn't mean that I think you're wrong; it means that we might have an interesting relationship. It might be very dull if all people thought the same way and liked the same things.

In this exercise you'll have an opportunity to examine a place where all people think alike, and so they all act the same way. You will be a student explorer on a just-discovered island, and you have to write a report for your college professor about what this land is like. In your report you call the island Sameland.

In Sameland everyone believes and acts the same and you have to describe what this is like. This country is much like yours in respect to language, so you're able to understand what the people are saying.

WRITING

Your parent might want to work with you on this paper. If so, you'll learn to share experiences and efforts. This will be good for you because you both have had very different experiences, and this should give you a good understanding, in a new way, of how people are different.

One of the first things you should do when you have to write a report is to make a list of areas you will have to report on. In this case you should think of what it would be like if everyone liked the same things and had the same beliefs. The list for this report could start this way:

1. Clothing
2. Food
3. Cars

If you work with your parent, you and your parent will have to go on with this listing. One way to think about this is for you and your parent to talk about what it would be like to spend a day in Sameland. Think about what you would do and what you would see.

Preparation:
You both can add to your listing after dinner when you both have had a bit of time to think about this problem. You can bring your additions in on day three.

Day Three:

Make sure your parent sees the additions to your list near the beginning of this session. While you're waiting, you can write the title and the introduction of this report.

The title should let your reader know that this is a report and give a general idea of its subject. It might read like this:

REPORT TO THE FOREIGN CULTURE DEPARTMENT
on the
EFFECTS OF TASTE RESTRICTION
on a
PEOPLE AND A CULTURE

If you and your parent cannot think of a title for this report, you may use this one, but it'd be better for you to invent your own.

In your introduction you should give your reader the following information:

I) **INTRODUCTION**
    1) The subject of the report
    2) Who authorized or ordered the report
    3) Why the report was ordered
    4) Who conducted the examination and what their positions are (jobs or ranks)
    5) What it was hoped the examination would show

A schematic (outline) of the complete report might look like this:

INTRODUCTION
1. Subject of report
2. Who ordered report
3. Why report was ordered
4. Who conducted examination in Sameland
5. What was expected of this examination

CONCLUSIONS:
1. Major Conclusion
2. Supportive Conclusions
    A.
    B.
    C.

    Support for Supportive Conclusions:
    A. (1st Supportive Conclusion)
        1.
        2.
        3.
    B. (2nd Supportive Conclusion)
        1.
        2.
    C. (3rd supportive Conclusion)
        1.
        2.

IMPRESSIONS OF INVESTIGATORS:
1.
2.
3.

Preparation:
    You're to have ready for day four a rough draft of the title and introduction.

Day Four:
>Make sure your parent reads your work early in the session. You're to begin the body of your report.

A report should be written so that the people reading it don't have to read more than necessary to get the information they need or want. This means that the conclusions of this type of a report should come first. An outline of the body of this report might look like this:

II. Conclusions:
>A. Major Conclusion (the one idea or piece of knowledge that is most important which is a result of your study)
>B. Supportive Conclusions (the minor conclusions that led you to your major conclusion)
>>1.
>>2.
>>3. (There may be as many as you wish.)

III. Support for Supportive Conclusions (what you learned that led you to arrive at each Supportive Conclusion):
>A. (1st Supportive Conclusion)
>>1.
>>2.
>>3. (As much support as you wish.)
>B. (2nd Supportive Conclusion)
>>1.
>>2.
>C. (3rd supportive Conclusion)
>>1.
>>2.

IV. Impressions of Investigators:
>A.
>B.
>C. (There may be as many as you wish.)

You should write the conclusions for this paper. The major conclusion might be that this land and its people are very dull and uninteresting. Of course, you may not come to this conclusion at all. You must come to your own conclusion. You will want to make a list of the reasons you came to the conclusions that you did. These will be your Supportive Conclusions.

Day Five:

Your parent will read your rough draft of the second section of your report (the conclusions). You should write the support material (section III, what you observed) for the first Supportive Conclusion. These support points will be made from your observations of life in Sameland.

One of the Supportive Conclusions you might have is that everyone wears the same color and style of clothing. In this case, all of the people would be dressed exactly the same way. If the favorite color were gray, all clothing would be gray. Both the men and women might like slacks and pull-over shirts. All people might wear lace-up black shoes. There might be large flowery hats on all people. There might be no styles or chances for individual expression in clothing.

Preparation:

You will have to write the rough draft of this first section of your report for day six, then start the second Supportive Conclusion and have it ready to show your parent.

Day Six:

Show your parent your rough draft of the first Supportive Conclusion. While you're waiting for suggestions, you should work on the next Supportive Conclusion.

Preparation:

Write the second rough draft of the first Supportive Conclusion and then write the second rough draft of the second Supportive Conclusion.

Day Seven:

Have your parent check your work. You're now ready to write the final copy of the introduction and the first Supportive Conclusion. You might start on the third one.

Preparation:

You should write the final copies. You should make ready for day eight the final copy of the introduction and the first and second Supportive Conclusion.

Day Eight:

You should work on the impressions of the investigators. This should not be just the same as the conclusions. This part of the report should tell your reader how you feel about the conditions found in Sameland.

I recommend you take the next week off.

PROGRESS REPORT

Name:_____ Date:_____

Exercise # 2 IF I WERE A. . .

Copy your best sentence for the week on the lines below.

_____

_____

Name one mistake you made this week that you can fix and will avoid next week.

_____

_____

Write the sentence that had this mistake in it.

_____

_____

Write the sentence again showing how you fixed this mistake.

_____

_____

Comments:

#3 CONFLICT

Sixth Level Skill Strand: Creative

It may take you eight days to learn that:
1. Conflict is one of the things that makes reading stories fun
2. You can create conflicts in your writing

PREWRITING

Day One:

Conflict is when there are two or more people or forces that want the same thing or want to keep the other force or forces from doing or getting what they want. Think about the most exciting parts of the books you've read. You'll find that those parts are the ones in which the conflict is most clearly defined.

This same situation is true in stories. People love to read about conflict. In fact, all stories are based on conflict because this is what stories are: incidents in which conflict is resolved.

In this exercise you'll have a chance to create a conflict and its outcome. This exercise has three parts. You will:

1. **Create characters**
2. **Put the characters in opposition** (conflict)
3. **Solve this conflict** the characters have

WRITING

You'll have to create at least two characters who will be in conflict. It would be best for you to create characters who are not alike. It would be easier to write the dialogue if one is a girl and one is a boy or one is an adult and one a teenager. Some suggestions might help you choose a situation and create characters:
1. A girl and her brother have to share doing the dinner dishes every night. The girl likes to wash so that she can leave the kitchen. The boy wants to wash so he doesn't have to hurry so much trying to keep up with his sister. They argue.

2. A boy gets an allowance each week, but he has chores around the house he has to do. He doesn't always remember to do what he is supposed to. His father has decided he'll "forget" to give his son his allowance. This causes conflict.

3. A girl just hates writing and doesn't do any unless she has to for an exercise. Her mother wants her to practice writing because she knows how important it will be for her in the future to read and write well. The mother and father talk to the girl during dinner about this need to practice using her language.

4. A boy wants an ATV. His mother is worried he'll get hurt.

Preparation:
You're to bring in for day two the point of view you will use in your fiction. It can look like the example below, but this isn't a suggestion that you use these selections. You should look in your file for the exercise on point of view to help you remember what choices you have. If you've not worked in *Writing Strands* before, you might turn to the fourth exercise in this book and read about these point of view options. Put the point of view choices you make at the top of your page. They might be put like this:

Point of View: Number: Singular, Person: Third, Tense: Past

Start on the descriptions of your characters which will be due at the end of day two.

Day Two:
You should have a situation and a short description of each of your characters written by the end of this session. This description need not be done neatly—it's only for your notes. It can look like this example:

Janet is 14 and very much wants to be like and do things like the other girls in her small town. She has a problem in that her mother has given her the family's values, and some of the ideas of the girls in town are in conflict with those values.

She wants to use makeup and wear clothes like the other girls, but Mrs. Smith, Janet's mother, wants her daughter to be a responsible young lady and not one of these crazy kids who thinks of nothing but music, boys and clothes all the time.

Preparation:
If you didn't finish your character descriptions today, do them tonight and have them ready to show your parent on day three.

Day Three:

Make sure your parent reads your work today. You should start on your conflict. If you're in doubt about how to punctuate dialogue, you should look in any novel or short story and copy the punctuation the author has used.

A few suggestions might help you get started:

It will be easier for you to create believable characters if you make them like people you know. You would understand some of their motivations, and you could even copy their speech patterns.

You should have your characters move about the place you put them, change their emotions to fit the changing situations they're in, move their bodies when they talk and appear to be motivated by their desires.

This is a lot and your parent may want to discuss these elements with you.

Keep in mind that these people move and talk differently when they're upset than they do when they're feeling calm.

You can show your characters' feelings by the things you have them do. Look at the example below:

Mrs. Smith was wiping off the counter in the kitchen when she heard Betty come in the front door and drop her library books on the hall table. She would have to talk to her again about not leaving her things all over the house.

Betty came into the kitchen and said, "Hi, Mom, any cookies?"

Mrs. Smith pointed to the cookie jar that she tried to keep filled. When she turned to look at her daughter, she noticed Betty was chewing steadily but looking intently at her. She raised her eyebrows and said, "What?"

Betty pushed another cookie into her mouth and said, "I'm going to get a job."

"When did you make this decision?"

"I heard you and Dad talking last night when I was clearing the table. I know things have been tough since Dad got laid off, and I wanna help."

"That's nice, Dear, but you have enough to do just helping around here, doing your school work and watching Randy for me. Thanks, but I don't think that's such a good idea." Mrs. Smith reached out and touched Betty on the shoulder and smiled at her.

"I'm old enough to help out, and besides I already have a job offer. Mr. Jenkins at the library told me he needed someone to help shelve books. I'd only make minimum wage to start, but every little bit helps." Betty spread her hands out wide and looked up at her mother.

Mrs. Smith said, as she turned back, "Well, the answer's no."
"I'm old enough to help."
"Not that way you're not."
"I heard Dad say we all had to pitch in and help out now."
"He didn't mean for you to get a job. You can't work and that's final."
"All right, but I don't see why I can't help."
"Things will work out. Now go put your books in your room."
"Okay, Mom." Janet turned at the door and said, "What's for dinner?"
"Liver."
*"Again? Wouldn't it be more fun if we were to have people food and
give the liver to the cat?"*

It would be hard, or even impossible, for you to write about things with which you have no experience, such as a conflict between two managers in a steel mill. You don't know anything about adult problems in business, and you can't know much about making steel. Write about people and things with which you're familiar.

Preparation:
Start your conflict.

Day Four:

You should prepare to show your parent a rough draft of the start of your conflict piece. There should be an introduction of the place and characters. Ask your parent to read what you've written so far, and work this hour using any suggestions given.

Preparation:
Rewrite what you have, using your parent's suggestions, and prepare for day five a second rough draft of the introduction to the conflict situation.

Days Five and Six:

By the end of this session you should have the rough draft of your piece done. Make sure your parent reads it before you start on the final rough draft.
You should have at least three pages of hand-written work by day six.
It should be about 600 words long. Have your parent read your work each day.

Days Seven and Eight:

Check punctuation in your dialogue against an example you have found in a novel. Have your parent look to see that you have done it correctly. Your final draft should be done at the end of session eight.

I recommend you take the next week off.

PROGRESS REPORT

Name:_____ Date:_____

Exercise # 3 CONFLICT

Copy your best sentence for the week on the lines below.

_____

_____

Name one mistake you made this week that you can fix and will avoid next week.

_____

_____

Write the sentence that had this mistake in it.

_____

_____

Write the sentence again showing how you fixed this mistake.

_____

_____

Comments:

#4 POINT OF VIEW

Sixth Level Skill Strand: Expository

It may take you six days to learn:
1. Some of the choices an author has in the use of point of view
2. How these point of view elements work
3. The structure of an explanatory exposition
4. That you can write an explanatory exposition

PREWRITING

Day One:

It may take a few days for you and your parent to work through the following explanatory material. There are two fairly complicated ideas here, but they're both very important. You must understand the structure of expository writing. If this is your first year working with *Writing Strands*, it will seem complicated. It is not. If you were to read a number of articles in *Reader's Digest,* you would find that the authors use a structure for non-fiction much like the one outlined here. You'll have other chances to practice this mode of writing, and you'll get good at structuring your writing this way.

The second important experience in this lesson is the point of view material. Don't expect to understand it all with the first reading. If you haven't worked with point of view material before, this will be new to you. Take it a bit at a time. It'll become clear as you practice it. Much of it's just logical and you already use it correctly.

A book or story isn't told to the reader by the author but by this narrative voice the author creates. This is a strange situation, but it's the way it's done. The author uses this voice to tell the story, and, in the creation of this voice, the author has a number of choices of the kind of voice to use.

On the next page are three of the choices an author has in creating a narrative voice.

```
┌─────────────────────────────────────────────────────┐
│                                                       │
│              THREE NARRATIVE VOICE                    │
│              POINT OF VIEW CHOICES                    │
│                                                       │
│     NUMBER:    singular           plural              │
│     ─────────────────────────────────────────────    │
│                                                       │
│     PERSON:    first     second      third            │
│     ─────────────────────────────────────────────    │
│                                                       │
│     TENSE:     past      present     future           │
│                                                       │
└─────────────────────────────────────────────────────┘
```

NUMBER

Singular,
First Person:

The narrative voice refers to itself as an individual and not as part of a group and uses *I* as in: *I saw the dog*.

Plural,
First Person:

The narrative voice, although speaking to the reader as an individual, constantly refers to itself as part of the group of characters in the story and uses *we*: *We saw the dog*.

Singular,
Third Person:

The narrative voice refers to one character at a time and talks about groups of people only in the sense of them being observed by one individual: *He saw the boy*, or, *She saw the mayor in the garage*.

Plural,
Third Person:

The narrative voice refers to a group of two or more people, using *they* or *them* as in: *They saw the boy*.

PERSON

First: The narrative voice tells the story as if it had been there and refers to itself as *I*.

Second: This is a very rare voice for an author to use. The narrative voice refers to the reader as *you* which puts the reader in the story.

Third: The narrative voice tells the story as if it had been there and it does not refer to itself or the reader, but refers to the other characters in the story as *he, she* or *they*.

TENSE

Past: The narrative voice tells about things that have already happened.

Present: The narrative voice tells about things as if they're happening at the time it's telling about them.

Future: The narrative voice tells about things that have not happened yet but will.

The following are examples of the uses of these three elements of point of view: **NUMBER, PERSON** and **TENSE.**

NUMBER: Singular and plural:

   Singular: *I saw the dog. He saw the dog.*
   Plural: *We saw the dog. They saw the dog.*

PERSON: First and third, singular and plural:

   First person singular: *I saw the dog.*
   Third person singular: *He saw the dog.*
   First person plural: *We saw the dog.*
   Third person plural: *They saw the dog.*

TENSE: Past, present, future, first person singular, third person plural:

   Past, first person singular: *I saw the dog.*
   Past, third person plural: *They saw the dog.*

   Present, first person singular: *I see the dog.*
   Present, third person plural: *They see the dog.*

   Future, first person singular: *I will see the dog.*
   Future, third person plural: *They will see the dog.*

This gets fairly complicated and your parent may want you to do some exercises or to study these options or even take a test to see if you understand these choices. You will write an explanatory exposition (a paper explaining something) on these three elements of point of view: **number**, **person**, and **tense**. You'll be writing lots of expository papers during the rest of your schooling, so this is something that you'll need to know how to do.

Definitions: **Explanatory**—the name given to expositions (essays) which explain the nature of things or how things work.

Exposition: exposing your reader to ideas or information (in this case with an essay).

EXPLANATORY EXPOSITION: An essay which explains something to the reader. The following material may seem hard to understand. Don't panic. It'll all make sense as you work your way through it. Your parent may ask you to read through this explanation and then may read through it with you.

STRUCTURE
for
EXPLANATORY ESSAYS

INTRODUCTION (has three parts):

1. **Background:** This is information the reader will need to have to understand the main idea (the contention or thesis statement). This can be a history of the subject or some personal experience and/or observation (more about this in a moment).

2. **Contention:** This is a one-sentence statement of position or belief, such as: *Chocolate ice cream is the best kind*, or *Growing up is exciting, but sometimes it's a lot of work.*

   This is what some people call the thesis statement. This is the point of the paper and is what the body will explain or show to be true.

3. **Process:** Usually, this is a one-sentence statement giving the order in which the body parts support the contention. Because this kind of writing is made up of *statement* and *support,* everything in the body must be related to the main idea (contention) in a supportive way. (Remember, don't panic.)

   These support points in the body must be in the same order as they're listed in the process. (This isn't that complicated. More about it in a moment)

Some examples should help.

I'll use as an example the planning and structuring of an explanatory exposition about how much fun it is to go to the beach.

INTRODUCTION:

1. Background:

We would first have to introduce our reader to the idea of having fun. This part of the introduction, called the **background,** might read like this:

One of the best things about living in this part of the country is being so close to Lake Michigan. When homeschool is over for the summer, all the kids like to hang out together and think of fun things to do.

2. Contention:

We now have to write the contention—one sentence that tells our reader the main point of our essay. For this example it might read like this:

The one activity that we like to do the most in the summer is go to the beach.

2. Process:

The process sentence will have key words that will introduce the reader to the support ideas in the body. These key words will be in the same order as the ideas are in the body. The key words will come from a breakdown of the contending idea.

In our example paper, about the fun that could be had at the beach, the key words in the process might be: 1) *swimming,* 2) *eating,* 3) *tanning,* and 4) *building sand castles.* (These four activities are the things that will support the idea that going to the beach is fun.) This **one-sentence** process statement might then read:

The things the kids like to do are swimming, eating, tanning and building sand castles.

This process sentence would tell our reader that we would be explaining about the fun that could be had at the beach by talking about 1) *swimming,* 2) *eating,* 3) *tanning,* and, 4) *building sand castles.*

The order of these key words in this process statement would tell our reader that the first group of paragraphs in our body would talk about the fun of *swimming*. The second group of paragraphs would talk about the fun of *eating*. The third group of paragraphs would talk about the fun of *tanning*. The fourth group of paragraphs would talk about the fun of *building sand castles*.

We would then have to put the parts of our introduction together:

> *One of the best things about living in this part of the country is being so close to Lake Michigan. When school is over for the summer, the kids like to hang out together and think of fun things to do. The one activity that we like to do the most in the summer is go to the beach. There we have fun swimming, eating, tanning and building sand castles.*

BODY: (has as many sections of paragraphs as there are key words in the process)

The body, supporting the contention, contains material presented in the same order as are the points (key words) in the process. This is so that the parts of the body—each of which may be composed of a number of paragraphs—will be recognized by the reader as supporting the contending idea in the order set up in the process listing of key words.

CONCLUSION: (has three parts):

1. The first sentence says the same thing that the contention does but does not use the same words.
2. The second sentence says that the information in the body is organized but does not use the key words.
3. The third sentence again talks about the ideas of the background.

In this paper you will demonstrate to your reader that you understand point of view by **explaining the various choices an author has and how each one works.**

NOTE—AGAIN: You will demonstrate to your reader that you understand point of view by explaining the **choices an author has and how they work.** This is what this paper is all about.

```
┌─────────────────────────────────────────────────────────────┐
│                                                               │
│         DIAGRAM OF AN EXPLANATORY EXPOSITION                  │
│                                                               │
│    INTRODUCTION 1. Background                                 │
│    (three parts) -->  2. Contention                           │
│                       3. Process                              │
│                                                               │
│                                                               │
│    BODY            The body should have as                    │
│    (in this paper -->  many sections of paragraphs as         │
│    four sections)     there are key words in the process.     │
│                                                               │
│                                                               │
│    CONCLUSION      1. Restatement of contending               │
│    (three parts) -->      idea (not same words)               │
│                    2. Mention of organization (do             │
│                       not use the key words)                  │
│                    3. A connection made between               │
│                       the body and the background             │
│                                                               │
└─────────────────────────────────────────────────────────────┘
```

REVIEW

INTRODUCTION:

1. **Background**: This material should explain the function of story-tellers and the idea of the narrative voice and that story-tellers have choices about how they tell their stories. Your parent will give you ideas about this part of the introduction.

2. **Contention**: The main idea for this paper should be that *the choices of point of view are not hard to understand or recognize.*

3. **Process**: the organization of this paper should be based on the *choices that an author has* in selecting a point of view.

In this paper the key words that you're to use in the process sentence are the choices authors have of points of view : *number, person and tense.* This means that you'll have to create a sentence that contains these key words.

This is easier than it sounds. Make a sentence with the key words in it in list form. It can be structured like this: *Most of the time I was at the picnic, I was with John, Bill, and Janet.* In this example the key words would be *John, Bill,* and *Janet.*

BODY:

The body of your paper will be organized on the basis of the key words in the process statement. This means that there will be at least one paragraph for each word.

The first key word in your process statement will be *number*, so your first section of paragraphs in the body will be about the point of view choice, *number*.

In this section of your body you should explain how number is used by the author and the choices the author has in selecting number for his narrative voice. Check again the chart showing the choices and the examples showing how each choice works.

You should use examples from short stories or novels to show your reader how the different choices work. If you can't find examples you might make them up.

There will be three key words in your process statement, so there will be three sections to the body of your paper.

CONCLUSION:

Your conclusion will have three parts:

1. The **contention restated** (Do not to use words that you used in the introduction.)

2. The **process restated** (remember <u>not</u> to use the key words). This is hard to do. Your restatement of the process could read like this: *An author has three elements available to create a narrative voice.*

3. A statement that shows that there is a **relationship** between the body of your paper and your background.

The background of this paper will tell the reader an author has choices, and the body of this paper will explain the function of these choices the author has. Conclusions are very hard to write, and your parent will have to work with you on this part of your paper. Do not begin your conclusion with the words, *In conclusion.*

WRITING

Work on the introduction. The first thing you should write is the contention—that statement which identifies for the reader the point of the paper. This will become the second part of your introduction. It could have something to do with the choices an author has when creating a narrative voice. Write it here:

_____

_____

The reason you should write the contention (the second item in the introduction) first, is because it makes no sense to introduce the reader to an idea before you know what that idea is. The next step should be the writing of the process. This is the third part of your introduction, and it will show how the body of your paper will be set up.

The process for this paper will contain these three key words:
1. _____
2. _____
3. _____

Using these three "key words," write the sentence which will become your process sentence here:

_____
_____
_____
_____

Background:

This part of your introduction must present to the reader enough information so that he can understand the contention. In this paper you might talk about what it means to tell a story. Remember that the author isn't the storyteller, it's the narrative voice which has been created by the author which tells the story. The author has to build the narrative voice from the parts available. Those parts are the choices of point of view. Write your background:

_____
_____
_____
_____
_____
_____
_____

Preparation:
You should prepare a rewritten introduction for day two.

Day Two:
If you're still having trouble with the introduction, make sure you ask your parent for help early in the session. You should write the first section of the body today. It should be about the author's choices of person for his narrative voice.

You should be able to find material in any book of short stories or in the library as examples to support your points. There should be one example for each of the choices the author has for a selected voice.

This means that you should find a sentence in support of the first point in which the narrative voice speaks in first person. Then you will have to find one in which the voice speaks in third person. When you have this written, make sure your parent checks your work.

Preparation:
Write the second point and rewrite the finished rough draft of the first point.

Day Three:
Ask your parent to read your second point today. You'll be writing the third point.

Preparation:
Write the finished rough draft of the second and third points.

Day Four:
Ask your parent to read over your rewriting of the second and third points. You should begin writing your paper's final draft. This means you will have to check for spelling and mechanical errors.

Day Five:
You should write the rough draft of the conclusion.

Day Six:
You will be finishing the final draft today. Give your finished paper to your parent on day seven.

If you've not finished with this paper by day seven, that's not a serious problem. It may mean that you're doing such a good job that you can't keep to this schedule. So what? We all work at our own speeds. The important thing is that you understand the ideas in this paper. If it takes you another two or three days to do that, that's okay.

I recommend you take the next week off.

PROGRESS REPORT

Name:_____ Date:_____

Exercise # 4 POINT OF VIEW

Copy your best sentence for the week on the lines below.

_____

_____

Name one mistake you made this week that you can fix and will avoid next week.

_____

_____

Write the sentence that had this mistake in it.

_____

_____

Write the sentence again showing how you fixed this mistake.

_____

_____

Comments:

#5 SURVEY

Sixth Level Skill Strand: Research

It may take you five days to learn to:
1. Write the questions for a survey
2. Learn to select the people to answer the questions
3. Take a survey

PREWRITING

Day One:

There will be three parts to this exercise: **writing** questions, **deciding** whom to ask them of, and **asking** the questions.

PART ONE:

There is a big business in this country asking questions. Some people spend years in college learning to get answers they can trust.

One of the biggest problems in asking questions is trying to write the questions so that the desire of the person asking the questions does not influence (sway) the answers of the people being asked.

This will make sense if you think of some of the questions you ask every day. When you ask your mom if there is going to be liver for dinner, she can tell by the way you ask whether you want liver or not.

When you ask your parents if you can do something, they can tell by how you ask whether you want to do it or not. Your best friend can tell if you really want to do something by how you ask about it.

Your parent may have some other members of your family ask questions and let you try and guess if the questioner really wants to know how the rest of the family feels or if the questioner is trying to influence the answers by the way the questions were asked. This exercise will be about how to write questions that do not to influence the person being asked.

28

WRITING

You're to write three questions that have to do with homeschooling in some way. They could be about the rules your parents have. They could be about something the family needs, like a chalkboard or a new desk or an air conditioner. They could be about subjects that you have to study or subjects that are hard to study at home.

To give you an example of how a question can influence the person being asked, I'll write two questions: the first one will be written so as to try and influence the answer and the second one will be written in such a way that I am more likely to find out what the person asked really feels.

1. *Don't you think it would be great to have all the houses in one block painted with the same color so that the neighborhood would feel more closely knit?*

2. *Do you feel that the houses in the neighborhood should be painted with the same color?*

Your job will be to write your questions the second way, without bias (influence).

Each of your questions should be written so as to ask for a yes or no answer. This way you will be able to figure out the percentage of the answers which are yes and no.

This is very hard to do and you should have your parent check each question as soon as you write it.

Days Two and Three:

PART TWO:

Surveys are given so that the people giving them will have an idea about how a large group of people feels or thinks about something.

Political parties, and manufacturing companies are two of the groups that hire large companies which take surveys for their customers.

These companies have to know that the groups who answered the questions were selected in such a way that they represented a much larger group.

As an example of how this works, pretend you're working for a company which writes and gives surveys. If I were to come to you and want you to give a survey in your youth group to find out if the kids like a certain math book, you would have to do one of two things: you would have to ask all of the kids in the youth group who were using that math book, or you would have to ask a sample of the kids using the book.

A sample means that you would have to select a small group of kids who would represent all of the rest of the kids.

It wouldn't be fair to me (your customer) if you were to ask only kids who have trouble doing math, any more than it would be fair if you were to ask only kids who find math easy.

You would have to select a sample of kids to ask which would represent all the kids: the good math students, the average math students and the poor math students. In this way your customer would have some idea how all the kids who use the book might feel.

Your parent will explain how to select a "representative" sample of kids from your youth group. You will have to select kids:

1. From all the different activities
2. From both sexes

You should make a list of the kinds of kids you will be asking. If you decide to ask 10 kids the survey questions, it might look like this:

1. 5 boys
2. 5 girls
3. An equal number of kids from each of the activities in your group (if there are 3 activity groups in your youth group, you will have to ask 4 from one activity, 3 from another activity, and 3 from the third activity). Make sure half of the ten kids you question are girls and about 1/3 of them are in the three groups, like this list:

1. Two boys   -   baseball team
2. Two girls   -   study group
3. One boy   -   volleyball team
4. Two Girls   -   4H club
5. Two boys   -   soccer team
6. One girl   -   volleyball team

Do not decide of whom you will ask the questions. Decide only on the type of person you will ask. This will be hard to do, but you will have to ask kids who are not your friends in order to get reliable answers. If you ask close friends for the answers to your questions, they might make a joke out of the exercise.

If how to select the kids to ask isn't clear to you, be sure and ask your parent for help in understanding it.

PART THREE

Days Four and Five:

This survey should be oral. This means that you should read the questions. You shouldn't let the kids being asked read the questions. You shouldn't answer questions they might ask about the questions or the subject.

It will help you to have the questions written on the same page with the list of who will answer them. There should be a place where you can write the answers. This paper might look like this:

1. Two boys -   baseball team
2. Two girls -   study group
3. One boy -   volleyball team
4. Two Girls -   4H club
5. Two boys -   soccer team
6. One girl -   volleyball team

1. Do you think that too much time is wasted on cleaning up after an activity?

yes_____   no_____

2. Do you think that clean-up time is well spent?

yes_____   no_____

3. Do you think there should be more of a variety of activities?

yes_____   no_____

I recommend you take the next week off.

PROGRESS REPORT

Name:_____ Date:_____

Exercise # 5 SURVEY

Copy your best sentence for the week on the lines below.

_____

_____

Name one mistake you made this week that you can fix and will avoid next week.

_____

_____

Write the sentence that had this mistake in it.

_____

_____

Write the sentence again showing how you fixed this mistake.

_____

_____

Comments:

#6 BOOK REPORT

Sixth Level Skill Strand: Reporting and Research

In this exercise you will learn to:
1. Identify the forces in conflict in a novel
2. Describe these forces
3. Show how these forces are important to the book

PREWRITING

Day One:

All stories, whether they're in short story, novel or play form, supply conflict as a main ingredient. This is what makes fiction interesting. We all like conflict. Even in dance and painting, conflict is important. Your parent may want to show you a play, a video of a dance or reproductions of paintings and talk to you about the conflicts in them. Or ask you to get pictures of paintings and have you point out the conflicts. Or, you might look for them together.

In this book report you will demonstrate that you understand your novel by identifying and discussing the forces in conflict.

This isn't nearly as complicated as you might think.

All stories have protagonist and antagonist forces at work in them:
1. The *protagonist* is a person or a force which must do something or wants to do something or wants something.

2. The *antagonist* is a person, group, or force which tries to prevent the protagonist from getting what it wants. (An easy way to remember this is that *pro* is for and *anti* is against.)

You have to identify these forces in your novel. Usually the protagonist is the hero. He or she will most likely be the main character in the book. The antagonist will be a group of people or a single person or a condition which will make it hard for the protagonist to get what it wants or needs.

WRITING

You should follow this outline:

1. Identify the book, author, publisher and printing date. This can read like this:

> *One of the more exciting books I have read this year is* The Long Storm *by Bill Smith, published by Simon and Simon in 1999.*

2. Talk about the book in terms of its conflict. This must be in present tense, and any references to the author, after he has first been introduced, should mention only his last name. You should write about:

   A. The forces in conflict
   B. The major characters in the conflict
   C. Where this conflict takes place

This part of your report can read like this:

(A)   *Smith centers his story around the old conflict between man and nature. There are natural forces that are strong enough to destroy men. Much of man's efforts have been to tame, control, live with or avoid these forces. Man has this intense desire to live, and to do so where he pleases. The natural forces have no will (they cannot chose how or where to be), they just are.*

   Of course, man has to struggle against these forces, just as Jake does in this story of a man caught in a winter snow storm in the mountains of the northwestern United States.

(B)   *Jake is a mountain man and has spent most of his life outside, living off the land and struggling against the hardships of his very difficult life. This makes him well equipped to survive a bad storm. He knows how to burrow under the snow and make himself a snow cave. He knows that he'll be stuck there for weeks and will have to eat his horse. He is willing to do this for it is a matter of survival.*

   The storm, the force of nature that Jake must struggle against, dumps five feet of snow on him and his horse. The wind creates drifts of up to fifteen feet. The wind chill factor makes the temperature far below zero. There is nothing Jake can do to escape the storm, but he must survive it.

   The forces in conflict are complicated by Jake making a friend of a wild wolf. The wolf helps Jake after Jake feeds the wolf some of the scraps of his horse. Together they survive the storm. This is complicated because wolves are seen as part of the natural force that man must fight against. This changes the forces in conflict to the living against the forces of the storm (nature).

(C) *Jake is caught above eight thousand feet. The storm is an early spring rampage of snow and wind. Jake is above the tree line and there are no caves or shelters. The clouds have been building for two days and when the snow starts to fall there is little air movement, but by morning there are two feet of snow and the wind starts to blow.*

The next section of your report should explain the action that leads to the climax. The climax is that point where one of the two forces in conflict must win and one must lose. This section might start like this:

The climax of the struggle between the two. . .

The last section of your book report should be an evaluation of the book. You should tell your reader whether you liked the book or not and why.

I liked this book because there are not a lot of talking and love scenes in it, and there is a good bit of action. The author explains how mountain men can survive, and gives details about tricks that make it possible to live under great hardship. That was very interesting to me.

I liked the part best where Jake makes friends with the wolf. I didn't think this was possible, but the wolf is also struggling against the forces of nature, for he too has been caught by the sudden storm.

Notice, in these examples, I have used the present tense in talking about the actions and characters in the book. This may seem strange to you but you must do it this way.

I recommend you take the next week off.

PROGRESS REPORT

Name:_____ Date:_____

Exercise # 6 BOOK REPORT

Copy your best sentence for the week on the lines below.

_____

_____

Name one mistake you made this week that you can fix and will avoid next week.

_____

_____

Write the sentence that had this mistake in it.

_____

_____

Write the sentence again showing how you fixed this mistake.

_____

_____

Comments:

SPELLING LIST

Every time you or your parent finds a misspelled word in your papers, write it in the column. This isn't a spelling drill. It will give you a running record of your problems. Ask your parent to check in the book *Evaluating Writing* for the process I recommend for learning these words. It's not nearly as tedious as memory work.

_____ . _____

_____ . _____

_____ . _____

_____ . _____

_____ . _____

_____ . _____

_____ . _____

_____ . _____

_____ . _____

_____ . _____

_____ . _____

_____ . _____

_____ . _____

_____ . _____

_____ . _____

_____ . _____

FIRST SEMESTER REPORT

WRITING SKILLS MASTERY

SIXTH LEVEL WRITING EXERCISES

Student:_____   Date:_____

Exercise 1. Body Control
Skill Area: Creative

Skill   Needs
Mastered Experience

_____   _____   1.   Understanding that adults are better than teenagers at controlling their body movements
_____   _____   2.   Using this understanding in writing

Exercise 2. If I Were A. . .
Skill Strand: Research and Report

_____   _____   1.   Understanding that the things we call good and bad (our tastes) are determined by our experiences
_____   _____   2.   Realizing that ideas may be looked at in more than one way
_____   _____   3.   Understanding that the organization of a report should help the reader understand it

Exercise 3. Conflict
Skill Strand: Creative

_____   _____   1.   Understanding that conflict is one of the things that makes reading stories fun.
_____   _____   2.   Creating conflicts in writing

Exercise 4. Point of View
Skill Strand: Expository

Skill   Needs
Mastered Experience

_____   _____ 1. Knowing three of the choices an author has in his use of point of view
_____   _____ 2. Understanding how these point of view elements work
_____   _____ 3. Understanding the structuring of an explanatory exposition
_____   _____ 4. Writing an explanatory exposition

Exercise 5. Survey
Skill Strand: Research

_____   _____ 1. Writing unbiased questions
_____   _____ 2. Selecting a representative sample as respondents to a survey
_____   _____ 3. Taking a survey

Exercise 6. Report
Skill Strand: Reporting and Research

_____   _____ 1. Identifying the forces in conflict in a novel
_____   _____ 2. Describing these forces
_____   _____ 3. Showing how understanding these forces is important to understanding the book

#7 DISORDER

Sixth Level Skill Strand: Reporting

It may take you six days to learn to:
1. Observe a situation and take notes so you can write about it
2. Describe what you have seen over a period of days
3. Write a formal scientific report

PREWRITING

Days One and Two:

Anthropologists are scientists who study the behavior of groups of people. Many times their observations are of what are called primitive people living on islands or in deserts or jungles. They make reports on what they observe about the customs of these "primitive" peoples.

You will be writing an anthropological report for this exercise. It will be based on your study of the customs of kids a few years younger than you are now.

You will be alone on this study. Often, when scientists go into the "bush," they have partners who share the danger. You will be going into some of the wildest territories known to man, the jungle of a gathering of children, and you would be safer with a partner, but some dangerous jobs have to be done alone.

This first session you will have to decide what kinds of behaviors you will observe and where this will be done and under what circumstances. Your observations could be made at a fast food restaurant, a sporting event, the mall, the local drugstore hangout, any youth group activity, or any place there is a gathering of kids a few years younger than you.

Remember that anthropologists study the social patterns of groups and are not so much interested in individual behaviors. In deciding what behavior patterns you will observe and write about, you might think about the list of possibilities on the next page:

1. The methods of entering and leaving the room:
   a) In a group or alone
   b) Skipping
   c) Walking
   d) Jumping
   e) Hopping
   f) Running

2. Communication before and during an organized point of the activity:
   a) Yelling
   b) Talking
   c) Whispering
   d) Note passing
   e) Sign language

3. Physical contact:
   a) Hitting
   b) Hand holding
   c) Back patting
   d) Hair pulling
   e) Object throwing

4. Activity during the gathering:
   a) Sleeping
   b) Talking
   c) Drawing
   d) Writing notes
   e) Paying attention
   f) Day dreaming
   g) Signaling to each other with:
      1) Eyes
      2) Smiles
      3) Notes or signs
      4) Gestures

Of course, what you select to write about will have to be determined by the place and the activity. Some of the items in the above listing will not work for a sporting event just as some wouldn't be suitable for an observation in the local library. There are lots of other things you could observe and write about. You can make your own list. Your parent might want to talk to you today about some other native customs and primitive practices that you might observe.

Preparation:

Tomorrow give to your parent:
1. The list of behaviors you will observe
2. The listing of places and events that you feel might give you a good observation.

WRITING

Day Two:

Write the introduction. This paper will not be like the papers you have written before. You will write this as if it were a scientific report to a university which has paid for your trip into the "Wilds."

You should start your paper with a title that tells your reader who the report is to, what group was observed and who did the observing. It can read like this example title of an observation made at a local fast food restaurant:

Report to the State University
on the
Eating Behaviors
of
Young Children From Middle Class America
by
(Bill Smith)

Your introduction might include:
1. The reason for the study (who wanted to learn what and why)
2. The importance of the study (what the scientists hoped would be the value of what was learned—how that information would be used)
3. The duration of the study (how long it took)
4. The general conclusions of the study (what was learned about the primitives—this can be in just one or two sentences and be very general)

You should be as creative with this information as you can be.

There is nothing wrong with telling your reader that the reports coming out of the "wilds" of the interior have indicated some strange behaviors of the "natives" and that your university has ordered you into the jungle to observe first hand and to write a report on these bizarre customs.

Your introduction might read like this. (Do not copy this introduction or paraphrase it.) Look at the four points that have to be in the introduction and then read how I have included those four points in this example.

(1)   This study of the eating behavior of the primitive people found in the fast food restaurant of (your town) was directed by the Anthropology Department of the State University. The Primitive Peoples Committee hoped that it could be learned whether it was possible that these primitives could control themselves enough to be trained to function in our society.

(2)   This is considered to be one of the most important studies conducted in modern times. If it is found that these natives can be trained, they can be used to run our factories, businesses, and institutions. If this is determined to be the case, schools will be set up to train these natives.

(3)   This study was commissioned on 15/342/2234 and took 13 durabops to conclude.

(4)   The general conclusion of this investigation is that there is no hope that this group of natives will ever learn to function in our society. (You may come to any conclusion you like.)

Day Three:

You should have the introduction written and the rough draft of it read by your parent.

The body of your report will consist of the conclusions you have come to and the observations those conclusions were based on. The list of behaviors you made on days one and two will give you the organization for the body.

Your introduction should present to your reader a general conclusion you have come to from your observation of the natives. The body will give your reader supportive conclusions upon which this general conclusion was based. This part of your paper might read like this:

Major Conclusion (stated in the introduction):

> *There is (there is not) hope that this group of primitive people studied in the eating room could be taught academic subject matter.*

Each section of the body should start with a sub-conclusion and that conclusion should support the major conclusion given in the introduction. The first body part can read like the one below:

Sub-conclusion:

> *The abilities of the natives to concentrate on their eating were found to be so limited and primitive that there is no hope that this group can ever learn the skills necessary to function as workers in a modern society.*

The investigators spent two days observing the eating behaviors and habits of the natives and found the following conditions:
1. 78% of the natives talk with food in their mouths
2. 15% of the natives hit each other.
3. 57% of the natives signal to each other with pieces of food in their hands.
4. 37% of the natives dip pieces of food in "red stuff."
5. 32% of the natives blow coverings off their straws onto the floor.

Other sub-conclusions can deal with areas such as:
1. Types of statements made
2. Methods of locomotion (ask your parent)
3. Methods of leaving the room
4. Methods of getting attention
5. Control of the rooms by the larger natives
6. Communication techniques with the larger natives

Days Four through Six:
There should be enough time in the six days to write at least three or four sections to your paper. There does not need to be a conclusion. When you have finished the last section of your body, your paper will be finished.

You will want to have your parent check over each section when you have the rough draft finished. When this is done, check your paper for spelling and mechanical problems.

Your finished paper should be given to your parent on day seven.

I recommend you take the next week off.

PROGRESS REPORT

Name:_____ Date:_____

Exercise # 7 DISORDER

Copy your best sentence for the week on the lines below.

_____

_____

Name one mistake you made this week that you can fix and will avoid next week.

_____

_____

Write the sentence that had this mistake in it.

_____

_____

Write the sentence again showing how you fixed this mistake.

_____

_____

Comments:

#8 INTERVIEW WITH A CHARACTER

Sixth Level Skill Strand: Report

It may take you six days to learn:
1. Imaginary characters sometimes do what they want to do
2. How to write an interview

PREWRITING:

Day One:

Newspaper or magazine writers, before they have interviews with people in the news, must plan their time carefully so that they can learn as much as possible while they're talking to their interviewees.

Good interviews are much more complicated than just the asking of a series of questions. There is research which the interviewers have to do. Reporters must find out all they can about people before they begin talking to them.

You will transcribe (write) an interview with a character from a nursery rhyme or *Mother Goose* story. In your research for this interview, you will first have to read the nursery rhyme or story so that you can know as much about your interviewee as possible. You will have to invent reasons why the characters act as they do.

When you think you know enough about the characters to be able to ask good questions in your interview, you should interview one of the main characters. Now your parent can help you. To give you ideas for your paper, you can play the character and your parent can ask you questions. For the written interview, your parent can play the character, and you can ask the questions. It's a good idea to use a tape recorder if you have one.

WRITING

After you have finished reading, you will have to do some research on the character for your interview. The outline on the next page might help you.

Name of the material:_____

Character's name:_____

What is the point or moral?_____

_____

_____

What part does this character play?_____

_____

_____

What makes this character do the things he does?

_____

_____

How does this character feel about the way things work out?

_____

You now have to try and think of the questions which will make an interesting interview. The following list of questions may help you decide the kind of questions to ask:

1. Who will your reader be?
2. What is your reader's age and reading background?
3. Will this reader have read the material?
4. Will this reader be interested in this character because of the type of character it is, or will this reader be interested in the moral or point?
5. What is there about this character that you find interesting?

When you have the answers to these questions, the questions you will ask your interviewee will be easier to write.

Day Two:

You should write the questions you will ask your interviewee (the character). These questions shouldn't be ones that can be answered by a *yes* or *no*. If they were, it wouldn't make an interesting interview because the questions would be longer than the answers, and your reader shouldn't be interested more in the questions than the answers.

The questions should be what are called open-ended questions—that is they should be written so the interviewee has to explain something in the answer. They should be written to read like these examples:

Q: *Old Woman, your family is the only one I have ever heard about that lived in a shoe. Where in the world did you get such a large shoe?*

Q: It must be very hard having so many children. How do you manage to take care of them all?

Write the questions for your interview here:

1._____

_____

2._____

_____

3._____

_____

4._____

_____

5._____

_____

Day Three:

You have written the questions for your interviews. Today you will ask the questions and your parent will play the part of the interviewee.

This means that you both will have to understand why your character does the things he or she does, and your parent will have to explain to the interviewer why the character feels as he or she does. This is the point where you can have fun with the interview. You can be as creative as you like.

I'll give you a *very short* example of what I mean. Your parent may want to review the story, *Little Red Riding Hood* with you so that you can understand the example. Your interview should have a short introduction like this one:

*An Interview
With the Woodcutter
from
"Little Red Riding Hood"*

I had just entered this small town on the edge of a large woods when I noticed quite a commotion near the village square. Pushing my way to the center of the crowd, I saw an old man with a bloody axe over his shoulder. After some of the excitement had died down, I was able to ask some questions of the old man.

Q: What in the world is all the commotion about, Sir?

A: I killed the Big Bad Wolf with my axe! Chopped off its head with one swipe. Course I had just sharpened it. When I was younger I could a done it easier even with a dull axe.

Q: How did you happen to do that?

A: There was a little girl lived here in town, name of Red Riding who used to go through the forest to see her Grandma Hood. She was a funny little thing. Wore red clothes all the time. A cape or something. Anyway, she got attacked by the wolf, and when I killed the wolf, out of the wolf's stomach jumped the little girl's grandmother.

Q: How did you just happen to be at the old woman's house to find the wolf?

A: I go there every Tuesday.

Q: Why?

A: I cut her some wood every week. She's got no one to do it for her. I got to get back to work, young feller. Nice talking to ya.

Days Four and Five:

Make sure your parent reads your interview today. While you're waiting, you should be writing the introduction. Notice, in my example introduction, that I indicated **where** the interview took place, **who** the interview was with and **why** I was interested in talking with the interviewee. You should include these three points in your interview:

1. Who it's with
2. Where it takes place
3. Why it's being taken

There is one final point that should be made in your introduction—you should describe what it's like where the interview takes place.

Preparation:

You should rewrite the introduction and the interview using the suggestions your parent gives you today.

Day Six:

Ask your parent to read over as much of your work as there is time for. You should start on the final draft of the whole paper. Turn in the finished copy on day seven.

PROGRESS REPORT

Name:_____ Date:_____

Exercise # 8 INTERVIEW WITH A CHARACTER

Copy your best sentence for the week on the lines below.

_____

_____

Name one mistake you made this week that you can fix and will avoid next week.

_____

_____

Write the sentence that had this mistake in it.

_____

_____

Write the sentence again showing how you fixed this mistake.

_____

_____

Comments:

#9 WHO ME?

Sixth Level Skill Strand: Creative

It may take you five days to learn that:
1. In some short stories there are stock or stereotypical characters
2. Some of the characters you see on TV are stock characters
3. In your writing you can create both stock characters and characters who have individuality

PREWRITING

Day One:

One of the things that good writers do that makes their characters seem so real to us is they give them individuality. This means that the characters they write about are not what are called "stock" characters. Stock means that the characters could be stored on a shelf, and the writer could just take one off the shelf and use it in a story.

These stock characters are often stereotypes. Some examples of stock characters who are stereotypes might help you to understand this idea.

There is the bad guy in westerns who drinks hard liquor, wears black clothes, uses poor grammar, needs a shave and is always looking for a fight. There is the tough and gruff but kindly detective, the hard woman who works in a bar who is really a very generous person, the young boy who isn't very popular but is a good student who uses his brains to solve major problems, the basketball coach who is a hard but fair father figure to the boys on the team and there is the gentle and friendly old grandfather who understands problems, and the other characters can talk to him and ask him for advice.

You can see these characters in your mind because you have read about them, or you've seen them on TV or in movies. They have become stock characters. When a writer uses stock characters, he employs the stereotypes that he and his audience are used to.

Your parent may want to talk with you about some TV characters who are stock characters and some who are not.

In this paper you will be creating one character who will be a stock character in a situation with more realistic characters. Here are some suggestions for stock characters:

- A mean and stingy boss who accuses a teenage worker of stealing money from the cash register

- A kindly priest or minister who solves a serious problem for a member of his congregation.

- The older kid, not a good student in school, who is always trying to get the younger kids to do things that are not good for them

- The lady who is so mean that when the ball goes in her yard she keeps it.

WRITING

You will have to create your stock character and the other characters that person will have to deal with, put them in a place and create a situation for them. Use this outline to help you:

1. Stereotypical or stock character type:_____
   Appearance:_____

   _____

   Stock mannerisms:_____

   _____

2. Where the scene takes place:_____

3. The situation the character is in:_____

   _____

Preparation:
   Use third person and past tense. Your narrative voice should be limited in knowledge to what a person could know. Your narrative voice isn't to be part of the action. You can decide to be either subjective or objective.

Days Two through Five:
   The easiest way to begin this piece is to describe the setting first and put your stock character in it. It might read like this **very short** example:

   It was late Saturday afternoon, and the piano playing in the Lone Star Hotel was background music for the last few families who had come to town to do their weekly shopping. The shadows from the short row of false-

fronted, wooden buildings fell across the dusty tracks almost to the board sidewalk on the other side of the street.

A lone horseman, pulling puffs of dust, rode from the west end of town. The still bright sun was directly behind him, and the people in town could see him only in silhouette. He sat low in the saddle and he and his horse both looked warn and tired.

He dismounted in front of the hotel, and the men sitting on the bench on the front porch could now see that he was dressed all in black. His hat was pulled low and it cast most of his face in deep shadow. The only part of him that was anything but dusty black was the buckle on his gun belt. That was Mexican silver.

His handgun was slung low on his right side, and the fingers of his gun hand were never more than an inch away from the handle as he moved to hitch his horse. When he stepped up onto the porch, his spurs rang loudly, for all movement in the street had stopped and the people, not talking now at all, watched in silence.

The stranger turned slowly and looked once back down the dusty street in the direction he had come, then studied each man's face in turn. The men on the porch shifted their eyes away and they did not meet his look.

The town had stopped and was watching him, almost as if the people could sense the danger in the stranger's slow but liquid movements.

I recommend you take the next week off.

PROGRESS REPORT

Name:_____ Date:_____

Exercise # 9 WHO ME?

Copy your best sentence for the week on the lines below.

_____

_____

Name one mistake you made this week that you can fix and will avoid next week.

_____

_____

Write the sentence that had this mistake in it.

_____

_____

Write the sentence again showing how you fixed this mistake.

_____

_____

Comments:

#10 CHOICES OF ACTION

Sixth Level Skill Strand: Creative

It may take you five days to learn to:
1. Describe a personal decision a person might have to make by giving that decision to a character
2. Put a character in a situation where the reader can see the character trying to make a decision that will be a good one

PREWRITING

Day One:

We have to make decisions every day and this must be done all day long. Most of them we aren't even conscious of, but some are very important to us and to those whose lives are affected by what we do.

I can make clear what I mean about the small and unimportant decisions we must all make by giving you an example of the kinds of decisions I must make sitting at my kitchen table reading a book. I might be drinking a cup of hot chocolate and reading my new Spenser novel. When I want to turn a page, I must make a number of decisions, most of which I'll have no conscious awareness of. Look at this list of decisions that must be made:

1. To turn the page
2. To use the right hand
3. To use fore or middle finger
4. To lick the finger or not
5. To use the thumb or not to hold the page steady
6. To use the rest of the fingers to help push the page to the left
7. To grip the paper lightly or not as the page turns
8. To push the paper all the way over to the left or to let it fall on its own
9. To straighten the page or not after it's turned
10. To select a place to rest my hand while I am reading the new pages

These decisions have to be made or the pages would never get turned, but the actions are so automatic that I don't have to think about them.

The decisions that are really important to life have to be made consciously. It's making these kinds of decisions that can mean having a good life that is dedicated to worthwhile activities and consistent with your values and goals and to the benefit of the people you care about.

Characters in fiction also have to make decisions. In the books and stories you're reading the characters must do this, and the authors had to think through those decisions just as you must in your life.

WRITING

Day Two:

You're to start writing a descriptive piece about a young character who has to make a decision that is an important one. This can be either a boy or a girl.

You can have your character make a good or bad decision. It doesn't matter as long as the decision is based on a value system. You might be more comfortable with a character with a set of values similar to the ones you hold. If this is the case, you will be familiar with the motivations of your character, and that is important.

This piece should have the following narrative voice point of view:
- First person
- Past tense
- Limited omniscience in knowledge (this is so you can show your reader the character thinking through the decision)
- Subjective in attitude

It might help you to have a short review:

- First person means that the author creates a narrative voice which assumes the role of a character and talks to the reader using the word, *I*.

- Past tense means that the author has his narrative voice speak as if the action of the narrative had already taken place. *Bill saw the dog*, instead of in present tense which would read, *Bill sees the dog*.

- Limited omniscience in knowledge means that the author has created a narrative voice which can know more than a real person could know in that situation. This voice can tell the reader what is in the minds of any of the characters. The narrative voice can tell what is going on or what went on in two places at the same time.

For instance, if the third person narrative voice in your piece is a non-character voice, then the voice can tell what the choir director said to Janet about her mother being ill but then can go on and tell what Janet thought about that.

56

- Subjective in attitude means that the narrative voice lets the reader know that it cares about what has happened to the characters in the story. A subjective voice sounds like this: *I was not happy to see Janet act this way.*

Your parent may want to go over these points with you during this session.

Preparation:

It may help you if you use this form:

List the kinds of things your character has to consider to make the decision:

1._____
2._____
3._____

Name the
character:_____

Day Three:

Start your narrative. Be sure and ask your parent for help if there are any things you don't understand about the point of view.

This paper can be just ten minutes in your character's life. You could tell about an incident when your character is faced with a decision and that decision has to be made right then. Your reader should see your character think through the options and apply a value system to the process of making up his or her mind.

Ask your parent to read your paper as soon as you have the first paragraph written. This may save you lots of work if you're not using the correct point of view.

Preparation:

Using your parent's suggestions, rewrite what you wrote today.

Days Four through Five:

Your parent will read your rewritten beginning and your new material and make suggestions. You should be able to finish the rough draft and write your final copy for your parent on day five. Make sure your parent looks at your paper before you ready it to present it in final form. This may seem like a lot of "looking at your paper," but there always seems to be some small detail that has been overlooked.

I recommend you take the next week off.

PROGRESS REPORT

Name:_____ Date:_____

Exercise # 10 CHOICES OF ACTION

Copy your best sentence for the week on the lines below.

_____

_____

Name one mistake you made this week that you can fix and will avoid next week.

_____

_____

Write the sentence that had this mistake in it.

_____

_____

Write the sentence again showing how you fixed this mistake.

_____

_____

Comments:

#11 PROBLEMS

Sixth Level Skill Strand: Creative

It may take you six days to learn how to:
1. Construct an argument between two people
2. Punctuate dialogue
3. Describe, in a dialogue, characters' major body movements caused by their emotional reactions

PREWRITING

Day One:

We move when we get excited, and we all get upset at times. It's how we move and how we handle being upset that tells others how mature we are. It's important to know what we do with our bodies when we get upset. This helps us to understand and thus control what we do.

We've seen characters in movies and on TV who have kicked and thrown things when they were mad. This is the way immature adults and some little kids handle their disappointments and frustrations.

When people are upset it affects their bodies, and we can tell how they feel by the ways they move. When we are upset with others, we would really like to blame them for how we feel, and treat them like we did when we were little, but we can't do that when we're big or we'd all be hurting each other all the time.

What some people do instead of striking out at other people is hit a table or desk. They kick at a chair or rug or yell at the dog instead of the person they're mad at. In some extreme cases, very immature people throw objects and break things like plates, tools and toys.

WRITING

In this exercise you will write a piece of dialogue in which you will create people who are upset for some reason. You will demonstrate for your reader, by what your characters say and how they move their bodies, that they're very upset. It will be

59

easiest to create people of different ages because the different ways they handle being upset will be so obvious.

Your parent may want to spend some of this first day talking with you about how and why people get upset and what they do when they get mad about something. You might want your parent to tell you of some experiences watching people who were mad.

Days Two through Six:
You will write a scene between an adult and a young person. This could be between a son or daughter and a parent. The child might be about seven or eight years old. You can have this conversation take place in the kitchen or in the child's room, or you can have the characters move throughout their house.

You will have to decide what kinds of people you will have in your dialogue. You could have the child not have yet learned self control. We all learn this skill at different ages. You could have the child get angry and have the parent remain reasonable and adult about the problem. This means that the adult would understand why the child is acting this way and know that the child is still learning self control.

The important thing in this exercise is that your reader sees the people use their bodies along with their words to express how they feel.

It should help you to get started if you first make an outline of the situation. You may use the outline below or create your own.

The names of the people involved:_____ _____

Where the disagreement takes place:_____

Who starts the problem:_____ Why:_____

Ways you're going to show your reader that the child is upset by having the child use his/her body to express this emotion.

1._____
2._____
3._____
4._____
5._____

One way to learn to punctuate dialogue is to pick any novel and see how that author does it, or you could look in the back of this book. The rules for this are very standard.

I have written a short piece of dialogue that I could use for this exercise if I had to write it, and you can copy how I have punctuated it if you want to.

> Bill said to his mother while she was doing the dinner dishes, "Mom, all the other kids are going to stay over at John's house for the weekend. There'll be lots of us there so nothing will happen."
> "Are John's parents going to be home?"
> "No, but they're gonna leave John's brother in charge, and you know how careful he is."
> "You can't go if his parents aren't home," said Bill's mother, as she took off her apron. "You should know that by now."
> Bill pushed his chair harder than he should have, and it bumped against the edge of the table. "I never get to do anything."
> "Well, this is one more thing you can't do," Bill's mother said while wiping her hands on the kitchen towel.
> Bill threw his arms out to the side and then let them slap against the sides of his legs and said, "Why don't you ever let me do what all the other kids do?"

Notice how Bill's mother has learned to control her body when she's talking to her child who is upset. Also notice that Bill is reacting with his body as a child might who has not yet learned how to handle disappointment.

Make sure you ask your parent to read your work every day. This is the only way you will improve.

I recommend you take the next week off.

PROGRESS REPORT

Name:_____ Date:_____

Exercise # 11 PROBLEMS

Copy your best sentence for the week on the lines below.

_____

_____

Name one mistake you made this week that you can fix and will avoid next week.

_____

_____

Write the sentence that had this mistake in it.

_____

_____

Write the sentence again showing how you fixed this mistake.

_____

_____

Comments:

#12 WRITING LETTERS

Sixth Level Skill: Organization

It may take you six days to learn:
1. The principles of business letters
2. The format of business letters
3. The writing of business letters

PREWRITING

Days One and Two:
This exercise has three parts:
1. A letter **to a company** from a customer
2. A letter **from the company** to the customer
3. A **letter back to the company** from the customer

Business letters should be:

1. Neat	4. Courteous
2. Short	5. To the point
3. Simple	6. Complete in information

1) *Neat* means that you should type if you can. If this isn't possible, the letter should be written in ink, have no cross-outs, have no dirty marks or smudges, be on unlined paper, but the lines of writing should be even and straight, and the margins should be straight.

2) *Short* means that you shouldn't say any more in the letter than the reader needs to know. Assume that the reader of the letter is smart and knows his or her job. Tell what you want him or her to do or know and let this person get on with the job.

3) *Simple* means that you shouldn't use long sentences if short ones will do. You should use short words and not try impress the reader with your vocabulary or your ability to write.

4) *Courteous* means that, even if you're angry, you will be more successful with your

letter if you're nice to the person reading it than you would be if you were not courteous.

5) **To the point** means that you should tell your reader exactly what will be needed to know to give you what you want. Come right out and say it like this: *I want a refund of $3.79 on the defective pen.*

6) **Complete in information** means that you should include in any letter all of the facts that the reader would need to know. If the letter were to be about a product that you had bought, you should include:

a) The name of the product
b) The model number
c) The price
d) The date of purchase
e) The store where it was bought
f) A description of what was wrong
g) A list of what you have done to get your money back
h) What you expect the reader of your letter to do about your problem

WRITING

PART ONE:

You will write a letter to a company complaining about a defective product you have bought and have not been able to exchange it or to get your money back from the store where you bought it.

Copy from a product in your home the model number and the address of the company which made it.

Make up the rest of the information on the above list.

FORMAT OF BUSINESS LETTERS:

Notice in the examples on the next pages that the return address in the upper-left corner of the letter is the address of the person writing the letter. This is followed by the date. Note that there are no abbreviations.

The address below this and to the left is the address of the person or company who is to receive the letter. There should be four spaces between these two addresses.

- There is one space between the second address and the greeting: *Dear Sir:*.
- There is one space between the greeting and the body of the letter.
- There should be a skipped line between paragraphs.
- There is one space between the body of the letter and the closing: *Sincerely*.
- There are four spaces between the closing and the typed name of the sender.

This first letter can look like this example:

333 Oak Street
Niles, Michigan 49120
January 10, 2001

Complaint Department
Pop Up Toaster Company
PO 182 Burnt Crust, Ohio 55843

Dear Sir:

On December 3, 2001, I purchased, in Bill's Appliance Store,
23556 Main Street, Niles, Michigan 49120, one of your
pop-up toasters, model number 4435. I paid $23.99 for it.

The toast does not pop up. Bill's will not exchange it or return
my money.

I am returning the toaster and expect you to return to me the
purchase price.

Sincerely,

Jack Smith

PART TWO:

Days Three and Four:

This next letter should be from the company to the customer. No matter how nasty a customer gets, the company representative must remain pleasant. Notice how nice the complaint manager is, even though the customer abused the toaster and does not deserve a refund. Write a letter like this one.

Complaint Department
Pop Up Toaster Company
PO 182 Burnt Crust, Ohio 55843
January 15, 2001

Mr. Jack Smith
333 Oak Street
Niles, Michigan 49120

Dear Mr. Smith:

We at Pop Up are sorry that you are not satisfied with your new toaster. We are proud of our products and would like you to be a proud owner.

Our engineering department examined your toaster and found the following conditions:
1. The toaster had been completely taken apart and then reassembled incorrectly.
2. Some of the parts are missing.
3. There are parts from other machines fastened onto our machine.
4. The toaster had been in a fire and was burnt beyond repair.

Our guarantee states that the toaster may not be repaired except by us.

I am sorry that we will not be able to return your money. We are returning your toaster.

Sincerely,

Fred French

PART THREE:

Days Five and Six:

This third letter will be from the customer to the company. In it you will insist that your complaint be taken care of. You must still be polite, but firm in your demands. Remember, you will be more likely to get what you want if you're nice. This letter can read like this example:

---

333 Oak Street
Niles, Michigan 49120
January 26, 2001

Mr. Fred French
Complaint Department
Pop Up Toaster Company
PO 182 Burnt Crust, Ohio 55843

Dear Mr French:

I am sorry your shipping department is having so much trouble, but I should not have to pay for their problems. When I sent the toaster to you, except for not working, it was in good condition. There has been a mix-up in your department of our toaster with another one. The model numbers are different.

1. We did not have a fire at our house.
2. I did not take the machine apart.
3. I did not add pieces to it.

I am a long-time customer of your firm, and I expect you will honor your guarantee now as you have in the past. I am sending the defective toaster back to you and expect you to send me a new machine by return mail.

Sincerely,

Jack Smith

PROGRESS REPORT

Name:_____ Date:_____

Exercise # 12 WRITING LETTERS

Copy your best sentence for the week on the lines below.

_____

_____

Name one mistake you made this week that you can fix and will avoid next week.

_____

_____

Write the sentence that had this mistake in it.

_____

_____

Write the sentence again showing how you fixed this mistake.

_____

_____

Comments:

SPELLING LIST

Every time you or your parent finds a misspelled word in your papers, write it in columns below.

_____._____

_____._____

_____._____

_____._____

_____._____

_____._____

_____._____

_____._____

_____._____

_____._____

_____._____

_____._____

_____._____

_____._____

_____._____

_____._____

EVALUATION OF SIXTH LEVEL WORK

Student Name:_____Date:_____

Writing Problems Needing further Work in Seventh Level:

1._____

2._____

3._____

4._____

5._____

6._____

Comments:

File this evaluation with your papers to be used with the seventh level work.

* * * *

SECOND SEMESTER REPORT

WRITING SKILLS MASTERY

SIXTH LEVEL WRITING EXERCISES

Student:_____ Date:_____

Exercise 7. Disorder
Skill Strand: Reporting

Skill   Needs
Mastered Experience

_____   _____ 1. Observing a situation and taking notes
_____   _____ 2. Describing what has been seen over a period of days
_____   _____ 3. Writing a formal scientific report

Exercise 8. Interview With A Character
Skill Strand: Report

_____   _____ 1. Understanding that imaginary characters sometimes do what they want to do
_____   _____ 2. Writing an interview

Exercise 9. Who Me?
Skill Strand: Creative

_____   _____ 1. Recognizing that in some short stories there are stock or stereotypical characters
_____   _____ 2. Understanding that some of the characters seen on TV are stock characters
_____   _____ 3. Creating both stock characters and characters who have individuality

Exercise 10. Choice Of Action
Skill Strand: Creative

Skill   Needs
Mastered Experience
____   ____ 1. Describing a personal decision a person might have to make by giving
                     that decision to a character
____   ____ 2. Putting a character in a situation where the reader can see the character
                     make the decision

Exercise 11. Problems
Skill Strand: Creative

____   ____ 1. Constructing an argument between two people
____   ____ 2. Punctuating dialogue
____   ____ 3. Describing, in a dialogue, characters' major body movements caused by
                     their emotional reactions

Exercise 12. Letter Writing
Skill Strand: Organization

____   ____ 1. Understanding the principles of business letters
____   ____ 2. Formatting of business letters
____   ____ 3. Writing business letters

LISTING OF COMMON PROBLEMS
with
DEFINITIONS * RULES * EXAMPLES

AMBIGUITY

A statement may be taken in two ways.

1. She saw the man walking down the street.

   This can mean either:
   A. *She saw the man when **she** was walking down the street; or,*
   B. *She saw the man when **he** was walking down the street.*

2. The use of pronouns *it, she, they, them* that do not have clear antecedents (what they refer to) can create ambiguous sentences:

   Bill looked at the coach when <u>he</u> got the money.

   This can mean either:
   A. *When Bill got the money **he** looked at the coach; or,*
   B. *Bill looked at him when **the coach** got the money.*

APOSTROPHE

An apostrophe (') is a mark used to indicate possession or contraction.

Rules:

1. To form the possessive case (who owns it) of a singular noun (one person or thing), add an apostrophe and an *s*.

   Example: *the girl's coat   Bill's ball   the car's tire*

2. To form the possessive case of a plural noun (two or more people or things) ending in *s*, add only the apostrophe.

   Example: *the boys' car   the cars' headlights*

3. Do not use an apostrophe for: *his, hers, its, ours, yours, theirs, whose.*

   Example: *The car was theirs.   The school must teach its students.*

4. Indefinite pronouns: (could be anyone) *one, everyone, everybody,* require an apostrophe and an *s* to show possession.

   Example: *One's* car is important.   That must be *somebody's* bat.

5. An apostrophe shows where letters have been omitted in a contraction (making one word out of two).

   Example: *can't* for cannot   *don't* for do not
            we've for we have   *doesn't* for does not

   Note that the apostrophe goes in the word where the letter or letters have been left out.

6. Use an apostrophe and an *s* to make the plural of letters, numbers and of words referred to as words.

   Example: There are three *b's* and two *m's* in that sentence.
            It was good back in the *1970's.*
            Do not say so many *"and so's"* when you explain things.

AUDIENCE

Writers don't just write. They write to selected readers in specific forms for purposes. To be effective, writers must decide what form is most appropriate for their intended readers so that they can accomplish their purposes.

Keep in mind that, just as you talk differently to different audiences, you must write differently also. You wouldn't talk to your mother or your minister the same way you'd talk to friends.

As you read your writing, think of who your intended audiences are and try and judge how what you're saying will influence those people.

Examples:

1. Informal—colloquial (used with friends in friendly letters and notes):

   Man, that was a such a dumb test, I just flunked it.

2. Semiformal (used in themes, tests, and term papers in school and in letters and articles to businesses and newspapers):

   The test was very hard and so I did not do well.

3. Formal (seldom used by students but appropriate for the most formal of written communication on the highest levels of government, business or education):

   The six-week's examination was of sufficient scope to challenge the knowledge of the best of the students in the class. Not being adequately prepared for it, I did not demonstrate my true ability.

AWKWARD WRITING

Awkward writing is rough and clumsy. It can be confusing to the reader and make the meaning unclear. Many times just the changing of the placement of a word or the changing of a word will clear up the awkwardness.

If you read your work out loud or have someone read it to you and then to listen to what they're saying, you can catch the awkwardness. Remember that you have to read loud enough to hear your own voice.

1. *Each of you kids will have to bring each day each of the following things: pen, pencil and paper.*

   This should be rewritten to read:

   Each day bring pens, pencils and paper.

2. *The bird flew down near the ground, and having done this, began looking for bugs or worms, because it was easier to see them down low than it had been when it was flying high in the sky.*

There are many problems with that sentence. To get rid of its awkwardness, it could be rewritten to read:

The bird, looking for food, swooped low.

Keep in mind that the point of your writing is for them to give your readers information. The simplest way to do this may be the best way.

CLICHÉ

All young writers like to use expressions they've heard or read. It makes them feel that they're writing like adult authors. Many times you'll use expressions that you didn't realize have been used so many times before that they no longer are fresh and exciting for their readers:

round as a dollar	*pretty as a picture*	*tall as a tree*	*snapped back to reality*
stopped in his tracks	*stone cold dead*	*fell flat on his face*	*roared like a lion*
white as a sheet	*graceful as a swan*	*stiff as a board*	*limber as a willow*

Usually the first expressions young writers think of when they write will be clichés. If you think you've heard of an expression before, don't use it, but think of ways to tell your readers what you want them to know using expressions that are new.

COMMAS

I am including commas because they are often seen as such a problem. Young people cannot learn all of the comma rules at once. Some will never learn them all. All writers have some comma placement rules they ignore. One thing that will help you is to read your work out loud and to listen to where your voices drop inside sentences. That is where a comma goes. This will work for about 95% of comma placement. This works because commas are needed and used to make clear the meaning in writing. They indicate a pause or a separation of ideas.

Rules: You should use commas in the following situations:

1. To separate place names—as in an address, dates, or items in a series
2. To set off introductory or concluding expressions
3. To make clear the parts of a compound sentence
4. To set off transitional or non-restrictive words or expressions in a sentence

Examples:

1. *During the day on May 3, 1989, I began to study.*

   I had courses in English, math and geography at a little school in Ann Arbor, Michigan.

The parts of the date should be separated by commas, and the courses in this sentence which come in a list should be separated by commas. Your have a choice of whether to put a comma before the *and* just prior to the last item on a list.

2. *After the bad showing on the test, Bill felt he had to study more than he had.*

   The introduction—*After the bad showing on the test*—to the central idea of this sentence—*Bill felt he had to study more*—is set off from this central idea by a comma.

3. *Bill went to class to study for the test, and I went to the snack bar to feed the inner beast.*

   There are two complete ideas here: 1) *Bill went to study*; and, 2) *I went to eat.* These two ideas can be joined in a compound (two or more things put together) sentence if there is a conjunction (*and, but, though*) between them and they are separated by a comma. Notice where the comma is placed in the example below.

4. *Bob, who didn't really care, made only five points on the test.*

   The idea of this fourth sentence is that Bob made only five points on the test. The information given that he didn't care is interesting but not essential to the understanding of the main idea of the sentence. The commas indicate that the words between them are not essential to the meaning of the sentence.

COMMA SPLICE

A comma splice is when the two halves of a compound sentence are joined/separated by a comma.

Example: *Bill had to take the test over again, he felt sorry he would miss the party.*

A comma splice can be avoided by writing this sentence in one of the five following ways:

1. *Bill had to take the test over again and felt sorry he would miss the party.*

2. *Bill had to take the test over again; he felt sorry he would miss the party.*

3. *Bill had to take the test over again, and he felt sorry he would miss the party.*

4. *Bill had to take the test over again: he felt sorry he would miss the party.*

5. *Bill had to take the test over again. He felt sorry he would miss the party.*

Notice that the punctuation of each of the above examples gives the reader a different idea about Bill and how he felt.

DIALOGUE STRUCTURE and PUNCTUATION

Dialogue is conversation between two or more people. When shown in writing, it refers to the speech or thoughts of characters.

Rules: Dialogue can occur either in the body of the writing or on a separate line for each new speaker.

Examples:

1. *John took his test paper from the teacher and said to him, "This looks like we'll get to know each other well." The teacher looked surprised and said with a smile, "I hope so."*

2. *John took his test paper from the teacher and said to him, "This looks like you and I'll get to know each other well."*
   The teacher looked surprised and said with a smile, "I hope so."

3. *John took his test paper from the teacher and thought, "This looks like I'll get to know this old man well this year." The teacher looked surprised—almost as if he had read John's mind—and thought, "I hope so."*

DICTION

Diction is the words chosen—your vocabulary as you use it.

Rules: There are at least four levels of diction:
1. FORMAL: The words of educated people when they are being serious with each other.

   Example: *Our most recent suggestion was the compromise we felt we could make under the present circumstances.*

2. INFORMAL: Polite conversation of people who are relaxed.

   Example: *We have given you the best offer we could.*

3. COLLOQUIAL: Everyday speech by average people.

Example: *That was the best we could do.*

4. SLANG: Ways of talking that are never used in writing except in dialogue to show characterization.

Example: *It's up to you, cook or get outa the kitchen.*

FLOWERY WRITING

You'll use flowery writing when you want to impress your readers with how many good words you can use to express ideas. This results in the words used becoming more important than the ideas presented.

Rule: A general rule that should apply is: What you say should be put as simply as possible.

Example: *The red and fiery sun slowly settled into the distant hills like some great, billowing sailing ship sinking beyond the horizon. It cast its pink and violet flags along the tops of the clouds where they waved briefly before this ship of light slid beneath the waves of darkness and cast us all, there on the beach, into night.*

This is so flowery that it is hard to read without laughing. It should be rewritten to read:

We remained on the beach gazing at the darkening sky while the sun set.

MODIFIER (dangling)

This means that there is nothing for the modifier to modify in the sentence.

Examples: *Getting up, my arms felt tired.* (How did the arms get up all by themselves?)

This should read: *When I got up my arms felt tired.*

Coming down the street, my feet wanted to turn into the park. (Again, how did the feet do this?)

This should read: *Coming down the street, I felt as if my feet wanted to turn toward the park.*

Being almost asleep, the accident made me jump. (It is clear the accident could not have been asleep.)

This should read: *I was almost asleep and the accident made me jump.*

PARAGRAPH

A paragraph is a sentence or a group of sentences developing one idea or topic.

Rules: In nonfiction writing, a paragraph consists of a topic sentence which is supported by other sentences giving additional details. A good rule is: A paragraph in this kind of writing should have at least four supportive sentences, making at least five sentences for every paragraph.

Example:

TOPIC SENTENCE: One sentence that introduces the reader to the main idea of the paragraph.

PARAGRAPH DEVELOPMENT: May be made by facts, examples, incidents, comparison, contrast, definition, reasons (in the form of arguments) or by a combination of methods.

PARALLELISM

Parallelism is two or more parts of a single sentence, having equal importance—being structured the same way.

Examples:

1. *We went home to eat and reading.* This should read: *We went home to eat and to read.* This is obvious in such a short sentence, but this is an easy mistake to make when the sentences get complicated.

2. *There are a number of things that a boy must think about when he is planning to take a bike trip. He must think about checking the air pressure in his tires, putting oil on the chain, making sure the batteries in his light are fresh and to make sure his brakes work properly.*

Notice that in this list there is a combination of four parallel participles and one infinitive which cannot be parallel in structure. (This sounds like English-teacher talk.)

What it means is the first three items on the list: (1) *checking,* (2) *putting* (3) *making* are parallel, but the fourth item on the list, (4) *to make,* is not structured the same way, and so this last item is not parallel in structure with the first three items.

This sentence should be rewritten to read: *He must think about checking the air pressure in his tires, putting oil on the chain, making sure the batteries in his light are fresh and making sure his brakes work properly.*

PRONOUN REFERENCE and AGREEMENT

To keep writing from being boring, pronouns are often used instead of nouns.

Rules: It must be clear to the reader which noun the pronoun is replacing. The pronoun must agree in case, gender and number with that noun. The most common error young writers make is with number agreement.

Examples:

Betty and Janet went to the show, but she didn't think it was so good. (It's not clear which girl didn't like the show.)

If a child comes to dinner without clean hands, they must go back to the sink and wash over. (The word *they* refers to "a child" and the number is mixed. This should read: *If children come to dinner without clean hands they should go back. . .*)

Both boys took exams but Bob got a higher score on it. (The pronoun *it* refers to the noun *exams* and the number is mixed here.)

Everybody should go to the show, and they should have their tickets handy. (The problem here is that the word *everybody* is singular and the pronouns *they* and *their* are plural.) The following words are singular and they need singular verbs: *everybody, anybody, each, someone.*

QUOTATION MARKS

Quotation marks are used to indicate exact words or thoughts and to indicate short works and chapters of long works.

Rule: 1. You should put in quotation marks the direct quotation of a person's words. When you use other marks of punctuation with quotation marks: 1) you should put commas and periods inside the quotation marks; and, 2) put other punctuation marks inside the quotation marks if they are part of the quotation; if they are not part of the quotation, you should put them outside of the quotation marks.

Example: *The salesman said, "This is the gum all the kids are chewing."*

Rule: 2. Put in quotation marks the titles of chapters, articles, other parts of books or magazines, short poems, short stories and songs.

Example: *In this magazine there were two things I really liked: "The Wind Blows Free" and "Flowers," the poems by the young girl.*

REDUNDANCY

Redundancy means using different words to say the same thing. The writer doesn't gain by this, only confuses and bores the reader.

Examples: *I, myself, feel it is true.*
It is plain and clear to see.
Today, in the world, there is not room for lack of care for the ecology.

This is an easy mistake to make, and it will take conscious thought for you to avoid this problem. You'll have to have help to find redundancies in your work. There are no exercises you can do which will help; just use care when you're proofreading your work.

SENTENCE

RUN-ON: This is the combining of two or more sentences as if they were one.

Example: *Bill saw that the fish was too small he put it back in the lake and then put a fresh worm on his hook.* (This sentence needs to be broken into two sentences by putting a period between small and he. It could also be correct with a semicolon between small and he.)

FRAGMENT: This is part of a sentence which lacks a subject or a verb or both.

Check your sentences to make sure they have both subjects and verbs.

Some writers use fragments effectively. You may do this in your creative writing. You should avoid using fragments in expository papers.

Examples: Fragments can be powerful if used correctly:

When Janet reached her door she found it was partly open. A burglar! Someone had been in her house and had left the door open.

SENTENCE VARIETY

Young writers have a tendency to structure all or most of their sentences in the same way.

 Give variety to the structuring of your sentences. A common problem for young writers is that of beginning most sentences with a subject-verb pattern.

Examples: *Janet bought a car. The car was blue. It had a good radio. She liked her car and spent a lot of time in it.*

These sentences could be re-written and combined so they all do not start with a subject and verb.
> *The car Janet bought was blue. Because she liked it so much, she spent a lot of time in it.*

SUBJECT-VERB AGREEMENT (number)

Closely related words have matching forms, and, when the forms match, they agree. Subjects and their verbs agree if they both are singular or both are plural.

Rules: Singular subjects require singular verbs, and plural subjects require plural verbs.

Singular: *car, man, that, she, he, it*

Plural: *cars, men, those, women, they*

Singular: *The heater was good.   The heater works well.*

Plural: *The heaters were good.   The heaters work well.*

Most nouns form their plural by adding the letter *s*, as in *bats* and *cats*. The clue is the final *s*.

It is just the opposite with most verbs. A verb ending in *s* is usually singular, as in *puts, yells, is* and *was.*

Most verbs not ending in *s* are plural, as in *they put, they yell*. The exceptions are verbs used with *I* and singular *you*: *I put, you put*.

Most problems come when there is a phrase or clause between the subject and erb.

Example: *This red car, which is just one of a whole lot full of cars, is owned by John and Bob.* (It is easy for some young writers to think that cars is the plural subject and write the sentence this way: *This red car, which is just one of a whole lot full of cars, are owned by John and Bob*. The subject of this sentence *This red car* is singular; there are just a lot of words between the subject and the verb, and it confuses the number.)

TENSE ERROR

Tense errors occur when past and present tenses are mixed and there is no justification for changing.

Rules:

1. Present tense is used to describe actions that are taking place at the time of the telling of the event.

   Example: *John is in the house. Mr. Jones lives there.*

2. Past tense is used to describe actions that have already happened.

   Example: *John was in the house. Mr. Jones lived there.*

3. Future tense is used to describe actions that will happen.

   Example: *John will be in the house. Mr. Jones will live there.*

TRANSITIONS

Transitions are bridges from one idea to the next or from one reference to the next or from one section of a paper to the next.

Rule: It will help your readers if you aid them in their reading by bridging their ideas for them. This can be done by:

1. Using linking words like: *however, moreover, thus,* and *because* and phrases like: *on the other hand, in effect,* and *as an example.*

2. Repeating words and phrases used earlier in the writing.

3. Referring to points used previously.

   Examples: If you were to write two paragraphs about pets—a cat and a dog, it would be necessary for you to make some transition between the two paragraphs—the one about the cat and the one about the dog.

Below is the ending of a paragraph about a cat and the beginning of a paragraph about a dog. The idea of having fun with the cat will serve as a transition to the paragraph about having fun with the dog.

> . . .and so I get a great deal of pleasure from my cat. She and I have a lot of fun together.
> My dog, on the other hand, gives me pleasure and fun of a different nature. We spend time. . .

VOICE   (passive and active)

Most sentences are built on the order of subject-verb-object. This produces an active voice. If a passive verb is used, it inverts this order and makes it seem as if the object were doing rather than receiving the action of the verb.

Your writing will be more forceful if you use an active voice.

Examples:

Active: *Bill threw the ball.   We must spend this money.   Bill drove the car with care.*

Passive: *The ball was thrown by Bill.   This money must be spent by us. The car was driven with care by Bill.*

Rule: You can use a passive voice if:

1. The doer of the action is unknown

2. The action needs to be emphasized

3. The receiver of the action is of more importance than the doer of the action.

Examples:
1. *When we were gone, the house was burglarized.*   (The one who broke in is unknown.)

2. *No matter how hard they played, the game was lost.* (The game being lost is the most important thing.)

3. *My pet mouse was eaten by that cat.* (The mouse is more important than the cat.)

WRONG WORD

The words you use do not always mean what you think they do.

Rule:

You should not try and use words in your writing that you don't feel comfortable with while talking. If you would never say the words *alas* or *to no avail* or *travail,* you should not write them.

National Writing Institute Order Form

		Qty.	Total
☐	**Writing Strands** Level 1 Oral work for ages 3-8 — $14.95 ea.	____	_____
☐	**Writing Strands** Level 2 About 7 years old — $18.95 ea.	____	_____
☐	**Writing Strands** Level 3 Starting program ages 8-12 — $18.95 ea.	____	_____
☐	**Writing Strands** Level 4 Any age after Level 3 or starting program at age 13 or 14 — $18.95 ea.	____	_____
☐	**Writing Strands** Level 5 Any age after Level 4 or starting program at age 15 or 16 — $20.95 ea.	____	_____
☐	**Writing Strands** Level 6 17 or any age after Level 5 — $20.95 ea.	____	_____
☐	**Writing Strands** Level 7 18 or any age after Level 6 — $22.95 ea.	____	_____
☐	**Writing Exposition** Senior high school and after Level 7 — $22.95 ea.	____	_____
☐	**Creating Fiction** Senior high school and after Level 7 — $22.95 ea.	____	_____
☐	**Evaluating Writing** Parents' manual for all levels of *Writing Strands* — $19.95 ea.	____	_____
☐	**Reading Strands** Parents' manual for story and book interpretation, all grades — $22.95 ea.	____	_____
☐	**Communication and Interpersonal Relationships** Communication manners (teens) — $17.95 ea.	____	_____
☐	**Dragonslaying Is for Dreamers - package** 1st novel in *Dragonslaying* trilogy (early teens) and parents' manual for analyzing the novel. — $18.95 ea.	____	_____
☐	**Dragonslaying Is for Dreamers - novel only** — $9.95 ea.	____	_____
☐	**Axel Meets the Blue Men** 2nd novel in *Dragonslaying* trilogy (teens) — $9.95 ea.	____	_____
☐	**Axel's Challenge** Final novel in *Dragonslaying* trilogy(teens) — $9.95 ea.	____	_____
☐	**Dragonslaying trilogy** All three novels in series — $25.00 set	____	_____

SUBTOTAL: _____

Texas residents add **7.75%** sales tax _____

U.S. Shipping:
$2.00 per book (**$4.00 Minimum**) .... _____

Outside U.S. Shipping:
$4.00 per book (**$8.00 Minimum**) .... _____

TOTAL U.S. FUNDS:

☐ CHECK or MONEY ORDER .... _____

☐ CREDIT CARD .... _____

☐ VISA   ☐ DISCOVER   ☐ MasterCard

Account Number

☐☐☐☐ - ☐☐☐☐ - ☐☐☐☐ - ☐☐☐☐

Expiration date: Month ☐☐   Year ☐☐

_____
Signature

(PLEASE PRINT) We ship U.P.S. to the 48 states, so please no P.O. #.

Name: _____

Street: _____

City: _____

State: _____ Zip: _____

Phone: (_____) _____

E-Mail (if available) _____

SHIPPING INFORMATION

Continental US : We ship via UPS ground service. Most customers will receive their orders within 10 business days.

Alaska, Hawaii, US Military addresses and US territories: We ship via US Priority Mail. Orders generally arrive within 2 weeks.

Canada: We ship via Air Mail. Most customers receive orders within 2 weeks.

Other international destinations: We generally ship via Air Mail. Delivery times vary.

RETURNS

Our books are guaranteed to please you. If they do not, return them within 30 days and we'll refund the full purchase price.

PRIVACY

We respect your privacy. We will not sell, rent or trade your personal information.

INQUIRIES AND ORDERS:

Phone: (800) 688-5375 TOLLFREE
Fax: (888) 663-7855 TOLLFREE
Write: **National Writing Institute**
         624 W. University #248
         Denton, TX 76201-1889
E-mail: info@writingstrands.com
Website: www.writingstrands.com

NEW ADDRESS